SAILING SHIP EAGLE

by
Barbara and Don Keeler

Crestwood House
New York

Maxwell Macmillan Canada
Toronto

Maxwell Macmillan International
New York   Oxford   Singapore   Sydney

Library of Congress Cataloging-in-Publication Data
Keeler, Barbara

    Sailing ship Eagle / by Barbara and Don Keeler. — 1st ed.
      p. cm. — (Those daring machines)
    Includes bibliographical references (p. 47) and index.
    Summary: The story of the U.S. Coast Guard ship *Eagle*, America's "tall ship."
    ISBN 0-89686-829-X : $13.95   0-382-24751-5 (pbk.)
    1. Eagle (Ship)—Juvenile literature. [1. Eagle (Ship) 2. Ships. 3. United States. Coast Guard.] I. Keeler, Don. II. Title. III. Series
V437.K44 1994
359.9'75'0973 — dc20   94-16736

Copyright © 1994 Crestwood House, Macmillan Publishing Company

All rights reserved. No part of this book may be reproduced or transmitted in any form or by any means, electronic or mechanical, including photocopying, recording, or by any information storage and retrieval system, without permission in writing from the Publisher.

Crestwood House
Macmillan Publishing Company
866 Third Avenue
New York, NY 10022

Maxwell Macmillan Canada, Inc.
1200 Eglinton Avenue East
Suite 200
Don Mills, Ontario M3C 3N1

Macmillan Publishing Company is part of the Maxwell Communication Group of Companies

First Edition

Printed in the United States of America

10 9 8 7 6 5 4 3 2 1

Created and Developed by The Learning Source

Acknowledgments
We would like to thank the many people who helped make this book possible. Our special gratitude goes to Captain Patrick Stillman and the officers and crew of the *Eagle*, without whose hospitality and patient explanations this book would not have been possible.

Photo Credits
National Archives: cover (inset), 9; Department of Defense: 29 (Official U.S. Navy Photo), 39 (Official U.S. Navy Photo); U.S. Coast Guard: 4 (Dan Nerney/Department of Transportation), 6 (center), 10, 41, 42, 44; U.S. Naval Institute: cover (center), 15, 18, 19, 30, 40; The Learning Source: 6 (top, bottom), 8, 11, 23, 25, 26, 27, 34, 36.

CONTENTS

Chapter 1 Under Sail............................5

Chapter 2 The *Horst Wessel*........................13

Chapter 3 Reborn from the Ashes...................17

Chapter 4 The *Eagle* Sets Sail......................24

Chapter 5 Across the Atlantic......................28

Chapter 6 At Sea with the *Eagle*....................38

Glossary....................................45

Further Reading.................................47

Index......................................48

CHAPTER 1

UNDER SAIL
NEW LONDON, CONNECTICUT
TODAY

With its engine humming quietly, the great white ship cut through the water, gently pitching up and down on the rolling sea. In the bright morning light, its sailors went about their work, doing jobs they had done hundreds of times before. Meanwhile, on the **bridge**, the captain and officers studied their maps and watched the crew below.

Like countless vessels before it, the ship was bound for the emptiness of the open sea. But this was no ordinary ship. In fact, it was a most unusual one for today's world of jet planes and nuclear power. It was the U.S. Coast Guard **barque** *Eagle*, a square-rigged sailing ship. It was not very different from the sailing ships that had crossed the seas hundreds of years ago.

Unlike the sailing ships of old, however, the *Eagle* was not carrying chests of pirate gold or crates of rare tea

The wind has powered the *Eagle* across many seas.

Eagle sailors went about their jobs expertly.

or silk. Instead, the ship carried **cadets** from the U.S. Coast Guard Academy. These young future officers were learning the teamwork and seamanship they would need in order to survive the rough and unpredictable sea.

Just an hour before, the *Eagle* had rested at its dock. Then, in a rush of activity, the ship had sprung to life. Heavy ropes—called lines—were untied from metal **cleats** and tossed over the side, freeing the ship from the dock. Marks were made on navigation charts. And the ship's engine, located far below the main deck, roared into action.

Slowly the officers and crew backed the 295-foot-long ship away from the dock. Then, carefully swinging the great ship around, they guided the *Eagle* into the deep water of the harbor. There the engine's roar softened to a dull hum, and the *Eagle* moved toward the open sea.

Now, with the land falling behind, it was time to raise the *Eagle*'s sails. The gleaming ship with the tall, straight masts would do what it had been built to do—be driven by the power and force of the wind.

"Sail stations!" a clear voice rang out. "All **hands** to sail stations! Prepare to set sails!"

Within seconds, groups of sailors gathered at the base of each of the *Eagle*'s three tall masts. Orders rang out from every corner of the ship.

Putting on safety harnesses and scrambling up the ratlines—the rope ladders hanging from the masts—the sailors instantly were **aloft**, 100 feet above the deck. Soon they were moving from place to place like circus performers on high wires.

Surely and confidently, the sailors inched their way out along the yards, the long beams that cross a ship's masts and to which the sails are attached. Then the sailors went to work, loosening the lines that kept the *Eagle*'s sails rolled, or furled, around the yards.

On the decks beneath them, other mariners went to their sail stations beneath the *Eagle*'s giant masts. In work crews of 10 each, they grabbed the heavy lines that held the ship's sails in place. Cries of "Heave...heave...heave" filled the air as sailors used all their strength to pull on the lines.

Length after length of heavy rope passed through the sailors' hands and fell onto the wooden deck. Creaking and snapping in the wind, the heavy canvas sails slowly rose into position.

As each sail reached its proper place, the sailors held tightly to the line. They strained to hold on as wind filled the sail and pulled on the line.

To a cry of "Back easy!" the sailors loosened their hold on the line, letting out a few feet of slack. Quickly, a sailor looped the extra line around a long wooden pin attached to the side of the ship. When the line was tight and secure, the sailor gave a cry, "That's well," letting everyone know that the line and sail were safely in position. Then the sailors dropped the line...and moved on to the next sail and line.

Within minutes, as cries of "Heave!" "That's well!" and "**Fore t'gallant** set!" echoed along the decks, half a dozen sails were up. This was just a fraction of the *Eagle*'s full set of sails. But it was enough to move the ship at a steady speed of four **knots**.

Work crews hauled sails into place.

If more sails were needed, they would be raised later. But for now, with a steady wind blowing, this was enough. Sailors came down the ratlines, and the crew moved on to other chores. Life on the *Eagle* settled into a routine.

Deck hands coiled lines and polished the brass equipment to a gleaming shine. Other sailors took turns at the *Eagle*'s huge wheel, steering the ship on a steady course. In the **bow** and **stern**, lookouts stood watch. Their eyes scanned the water for nearby ships, approaching storms, and dangerous floating debris.

Other sailors used the sun to **plot** the ship's position on the open sea. Every few minutes they reported their findings to the navigation crew, which traced the *Eagle*'s movements on detailed maps and charts. Watching weather and wind—as well as the computers and radio equipment in the chart house behind them—the navigators kept the ship on course toward its destination.

Sailors swiftly scrambled up the *Eagle*'s tall masts.

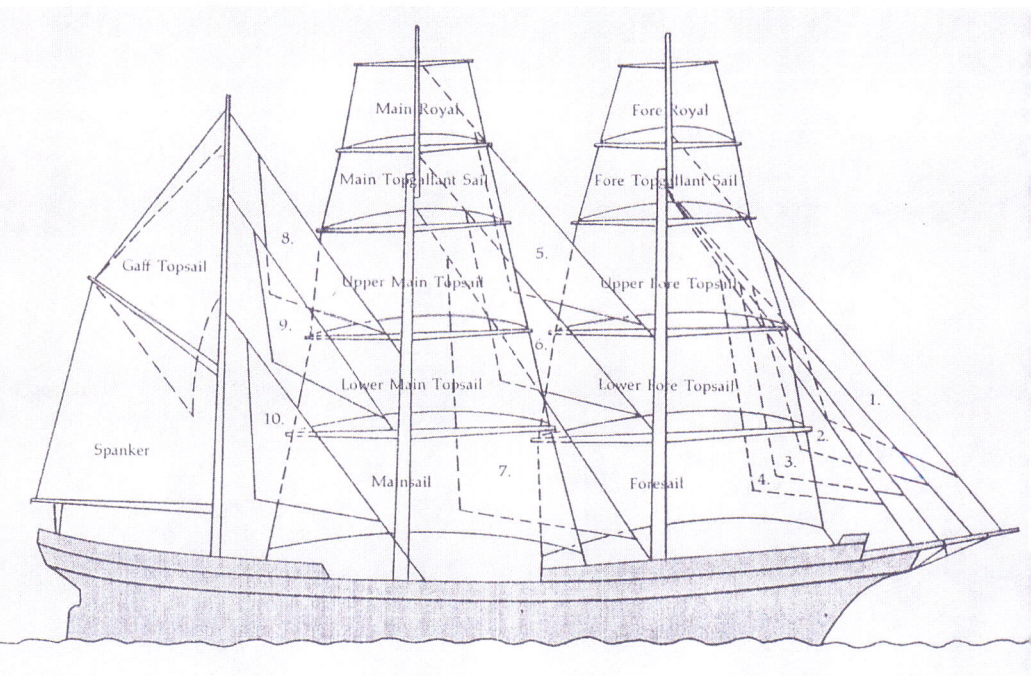

From the first, each part of the *Eagle*'s sail plan has had a job and a name.

Meanwhile, drills kept the officers and crew prepared for any emergency. Fire drills, person-overboard drills, collision drills—all were done again and again. Soon every member of the crew knew exactly what he or she was supposed to do in case of an emergency.

Bells announced the passing hours. Every four hours, **watches** changed, and the sailors switched jobs or took time to relax.

As the hours passed, the ship's loudspeakers announced more drills or called individual sailors to special duties. Every once in a while, the announcements ordered the crew to sail stations.

At their sail stations, work crews raised or lowered sails to adjust the *Eagle*'s speed. Sometimes they would **wear ship**. This was a complicated maneuver that needed the labor of dozens of sailors. Hauling on the lines once again, the sailors shifted the yards on the masts, matching the angle of the sails to the wind to change the ship's course or respond to a change in the direction of the wind.

At midday and sunset, sailors formed small groups and filed into the crew's **mess** to get heaping plates of food dished out by the cook's crew. Then, a deck below, they sat at long tables, sharing their meals and companionship with other members of the crew. Meanwhile, the ship's officers enjoyed a more

Work crews were busy with navigation and steering.

formal meal aft, toward the stern of the ship. In a **ward room** decorated with souvenirs of the *Eagle*'s past, they ate and swapped stories of life at sea.

Hour after hour, the work went on. At night, the call to sail stations woke sleeping sailors in their bunks. Groping their way on deck, the sailors worked in the harsh glare of the spotlights that lit up the *Eagle*'s decks and sails. Then, their work done, they staggered back down to their bunks, hoping for a few more hours of sleep.

For other people, the work might seem hard and the sameness of the routines might be boring. But for the men and women of the *Eagle*, even the smallest detail was important. How to judge the wind, how to tie a knot, how to place a foot on a ratline—all were necessary parts of their training. And all might someday help them keep a ship afloat on a dangerous sea.

THE *HORST WESSEL*
GERMANY
1945

There have been ships named *Eagle* in the U.S. Coast Guard since the service's beginnings in 1790. But the story of this, the sixth Coast Guard *Eagle*, does not begin in the United States. Instead, it starts thousands of miles and half a century away, in the ashes and rubble of Adolf Hitler's Germany.

In 1945, World War II drew to an end. The Allies—the United States, Britain, France, the Soviet Union, and other nations—had finally defeated the German forces. Germany had been invaded and conquered. Much of the country lay in ruins, destroyed by bombs, tanks, and artillery shells.

Among the **spoils of war** claimed by the Allies was a most unusual ship. Built in 1936, it was named for Horst Wessel (pronounced horst VES-il), an early and very

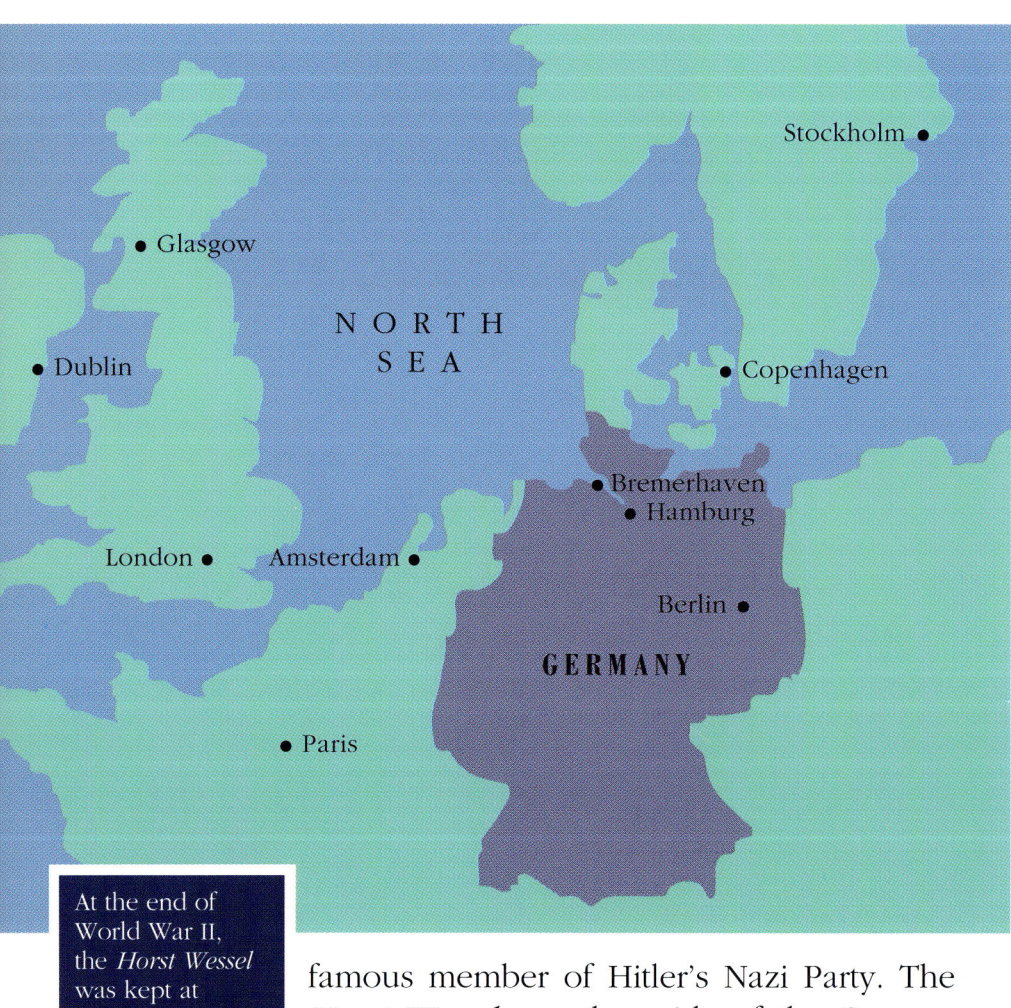

At the end of World War II, the *Horst Wessel* was kept at Bremerhaven, in northern Germany.

famous member of Hitler's Nazi Party. The *Horst Wessel* was the pride of the German navy. But it was not a fighting ship. It was a three-masted sailing ship, built to train German naval officers in the ways of the sea.

During the war, the *Horst Wessel* carried people and supplies from place to place. It even had a few minor skirmishes — short fights — with Allied forces.

At war's end, the *Horst Wessel* lay at a dock in Bremerhaven, one of Germany's important ports. The ship was in a sorry state. With supplies hard to find in war-torn Germany, the ship had had few repairs in recent years. Even normal maintenance had been skipped.

The *Horst Wessel* was built to train German naval cadets.

Still, the U.S. Coast Guard was interested in getting the *Horst Wessel*. Like many other seagoing services around the world, the Coast Guard had a long tradition of training its officers aboard sailing ships.

To the Coast Guard, the experience of being "under sail" was important for cadets. Being under sail gave young men and women confidence. It taught them how to handle a ship in everything from gentle breezes to fierce storms. But most of all, it taught cadets how to live and work together — all types of people, in all sorts of difficult conditions.

In 1945, the Coast Guard took possession of the German training ship. The Coast Guard then sent Commander Gordon McGowan to Germany to take charge of the *Horst Wessel* and bring it to the United States. What the young Coast Guard officer found, however, surprised him.

CHAPTER 3

REBORN FROM THE ASHES
BREMERHAVEN, GERMANY
1946

Commander McGowan arrived in Bremerhaven during the winter of 1946. Within hours he made his way to the bombed-out shipyard where the *Horst Wessel* was docked. He tramped across the grounds, picking his way through the shattered buildings and piles of rubble. When he reached the water's edge, he could only stare in shock at his new command.

The rusting ship rested in the mud of low tide. Stains covered its gray sides, and its paint was cracked and blistered. The ship's towering masts leaned to the side like giant, wind-battered trees about to crash to the ground.

Getting closer, McGowan could see patches and tatters on the huge, square sails. He shook his head as he scanned the worn-out rigging. How could he trust those lines and wires to hold up the giant masts and control the giant sails?

The *Horst Wessel* lay among the ruins of Bremerhaven.

Besides, sailors would need to climb that rigging to get to the tops of the masts. How could he order crew members to risk their lives on such worn-out lines?

McGowan's surprises, however, were not over. After boarding the ship, he had still another shock. One by one he searched the ship's holds, the storage areas below the main deck. They were bare! There were no tools, no spare parts, no supplies of any kind. Even the ship's engine was damaged so badly that the entire thing would have to be replaced.

At the helm, the main steering station, McGowan found three huge steering wheels. They were mounted on a single shaft so that when a sailor turned one wheel, the others would turn with it. But, though he tried with all his strength, McGowan couldn't budge the wheels. Something was seriously wrong with the ship's steering, too.

That was not all. During the war, a bomb had narrowly missed the ship. The nearby explosion had damaged the *Horst Wessel*'s rudder. The rudder, which was needed to steer the giant ship, would hardly turn. And since the ship had not been hauled out of the water since the bombing, nobody knew how badly the ship's bottom was damaged, either.

This was the vessel McGowan was supposed to sail across the Atlantic! The amount of work to be done before that could happen was staggering.

Work quickly began on the former German ship.

McGowan quickly did some figuring. To repair the ship's rigging would take more than 22 miles of line. And more would be needed for spares. Thousands of other items needed repair—or replacement. But where would the parts and supplies come from? During the war, most of Bremerhaven had been destroyed by Allied bombs. Not many usable supplies remained.

To make matters worse, McGowan didn't have people—or money—to make the repairs. His orders declared that he was not to spend a single cent of American money on the project. As a result, he would have to rely on workers he could have for free—a handful of American sailors, part of the ship's former German crew, and a few half-starved civilian workers from the shipyard.

Gordon McGowan, however, was not a person to give up in the face of a challenge. He immediately set to work, determined to do the best he could.

One of his first acts was to make friends with what was left of the *Horst Wessel*'s German crew.

The German captain was called *Ka-Leut*, short for *Kapitan-Leutnant*, the man's rank in the old German navy. Within days, Ka-Leut and his sailors were showing McGowan how the *Horst Wessel* was run—and exactly what would be needed to get the ship repaired.

Next, McGowan and his workers began to search the countryside for supplies. Other people—Allied soldiers and German civilians alike—were doing much the same thing. After all, just about everything was in short supply in postwar Germany. But McGowan and his crew quickly became a clever and sometimes greedy gang. Their successes were surprising.

One day, for example, McGowan heard rumors of a German naval warehouse still standing in an area that had not been heavily bombed. Who knew what treasures lay inside?

McGowan rushed to the warehouse and convinced its guard to let him in. Entering the building, the American squinted and finally was able to see some dusty piles. As his eyes grew more used to the dim light, McGowan could see row after row of neatly coiled rope. Excitement bubbling up inside him, he walked down the rows. He had found a treasure indeed—miles and miles of rope and wire. It would be more than enough to replace the ragged rigging of the *Horst Wessel*.

There was more, announced the building's guard. The man led McGowan to the basement. There, a familiar smell made its way to McGowan's nostrils. It was a mixture of salt, pine tar, and rope—tarred oak and hemp. It was just the thing he needed to fill cracks in the *Horst Wessel*'s wooden decks!

McGowan had one problem, though. The supplies in the warehouse weren't his. And there were other people who would want them, too. How was he to get what he needed before word of the warehouse's contents leaked out?

On the way back to the *Horst Wessel*, McGowan stopped to visit his commanding officer. Casually, he mentioned the problems he was having getting supplies for free. The solution, McGowan suggested, was simple. He should be allowed to round up what he needed—without having to pay for it.

To McGowan's surprise, his superior officer agreed, giving him permission to take whatever he could find—within reason. He even wished the clever young man "good hunting!"

Pleased with himself, McGowan raced back to his ship. Soon his crew was carting the badly needed supplies away from the warehouse.

McGowan was not the only member of the *Horst Wessel*'s crew who was skilled at getting material. The ship's supply officer, known as Von, quickly proved even better at this than his captain!

Although he had been raised in the United States, Von had been born in Germany. He spoke German like a native and immediately put his skill to use. As the days passed, Von became a familiar sight around Bremerhaven, **wheeling and dealing** for whatever the ship needed.

To find sailcloth, Von traveled far into the heartland of Germany. There he found enough to replace every sail on the ship...with plenty left to spare. A few days later, he located miles of twine, enough to last the ship for many years. Thanks to Von, sail makers were soon hard at work, sewing the ship a brand-new set of sails.

One problem, however, still remained. The *Horst Wessel*'s engine was a disaster. There was no choice but to get a new one. Where could McGowan possibly find it?

The factory that had built the ship's original engine was still working. But it was now under British control. And the British wanted the factory's engines for themselves.

McGowan talked to the British officer in charge of the engine factory. For a while it seemed that nothing would convince him that fixing up a broken-down sailing ship was important.

Suddenly, however, the British officer noticed the Coast Guard badges on McGowan's uniform. He told McGowan that he had seen the Coast Guard in action when the Allies had launched their invasion of Europe at the Normandy beaches, in France. He was glad, the British officer announced, to help the service that had saved so many British fliers whose planes had been shot down during the battle. If the Coast Guard needed an engine, it could have one!

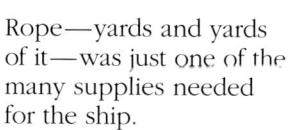

Rope—yards and yards of it—was just one of the many supplies needed for the ship.

CHAPTER 4

THE *EAGLE* SETS SAIL
BREMERHAVEN, GERMANY
1946

With a new engine on the way, McGowan's spirits lifted. Even though problem after problem arose, the crew and the young skipper somehow managed to find solutions.

To deal with the ship's broken rudder and rusting **hull**, the *Horst Wessel* was lifted out of the water. The rudder was repaired. Then, using high-pressure hoses, workers blasted away at the mud and **barnacles** that covered the hull. Soon the hull and its graceful lines were clearly visible for all to admire.

The workers and crew next attacked the ship's rust-stained paint. Rust and old paint were scraped away. With paint found by the ever-clever Von, the drab gray of the German navy was replaced by the bright, gleaming white of the U.S. Coast Guard.

With his ship nearly finished, McGowan had only one major problem left—a crew. The *Horst Wessel* usually carried a crew of 369—and the ship needed every one of them. Just about every task on board was done by hand, from raising and lowering the sails to lifting the ship's giant anchor. (It took 40 crew members just to do that job!)

For weeks, McGowan had been expecting more crew members to arrive from the Coast Guard. To his shock, however, the Coast Guard suddenly announced that no more sailors were available.

McGowan was at a loss. Right now, he had a crew of just 50. To make matters worse, many of the Americans who had been sent to the *Horst Wessel* had not been to sea before!

McGowan knew the situation was a recipe for disaster. For a time, it seemed hopeless. McGowan couldn't even hire the Germans from the ship's former crew because of the Coast Guard's orders not to spend American money on the ship.

Lines and ropes crowded the deck of the *Eagle*.

Once again, however, luck went McGowan's way. One day he was talking with the British naval officer in charge of clearing the North Sea of German **mines**. He had hundreds of German sailors working with him on the job, many of whom were experienced square-rig sailors. And, to McGowan's delight, the British officer needed even more sailors!

The Coast Guard skipper and the British officer soon worked out a deal. The *Horst Wessel*'s German crew would be hired for mine-clearing duty in the North Sea. But before they actually began work, they — and other experienced German sailors — would be temporarily sent back to the *Horst Wessel*. McGowan could use them to make repairs or even to sail across the Atlantic. Best of all, the sailors would be paid by the British navy the whole time.

Both officers were pleased with the arrangement. The British got the mine-clearing sailors they needed. And the Americans got their square-rig sailors — at no cost to the Coast Guard.

Stays that supported the masts and sails lined the sides of the *Eagle*.

The ship was named *Eagle* after a long line of Coast Guard vessels.

On May 15, 1946, a ceremony welcomed the former *Horst Wessel* into American service. The U.S. flag was raised over the ship's stern, and the ship that had trained Nazi sailors officially became the U.S. Coast Guard barque *Eagle*.

The next two weeks sped by. The new sails were completed and put in place. The crew scampered about the rigging, learning their ship and their jobs at once.

On May 30, the day set for the *Eagle*'s voyage, all was ready — all, that is, except the wind. The day dawned bright and sunny, but without enough breeze to power the ship's great canvas sails. So, its engine roaring, the *Eagle* left Bremerhaven under power, bound for a new life in a new country.

CHAPTER 5

ACROSS THE ATLANTIC
FROM BREMERHAVEN TO NEW YORK
1946

The first leg of the *Eagle*'s journey took it from Bremerhaven to Falmouth, in the south of England. Normally, it would have been a good chance for the *Eagle*'s crew to settle in and get used to sailing their ship. But it was not to be.

Throughout the trip, the wind blew either too weakly or from the wrong direction. As a result, the *Eagle*'s sails remained furled on the yards, and the ship made its way under power. The trip was dull, uncomfortable, and cold. But at least the *Eagle*'s voyage to its new home had begun.

In Falmouth, the *Eagle*'s crew waited impatiently. A fierce storm raged across the coast of England. To keep out of its way, the *Eagle* stayed in port an extra four days.

During the time in port, crowds flocked to see the majestic ship. Small boats soon surrounded the *Eagle*,

The *Eagle*'s engine powered it on its first—and many other—voyages.

bringing passengers out into the harbor for a closer look at the ship.

The admiring looks went to the heads of some of the younger members of the *Eagle*'s crew. Soon they were swaggering around like **old salts**. Every so often, they shouted out one of the sailing terms they had just learned— louder than necessary. Then, with a hitch in their walks, they made their way along the deck, lords of the sea and masters of one of the last great sailing ships on earth.

> Wind filled the sails and drove the *Eagle* across the sea.

Finally, with the storms gone, the *Eagle* set out once again. A powerboat traveling from England to New York usually headed directly across the Atlantic. However, like hundreds of sailing ships before it, the *Eagle* headed south, toward the island of Madeira, off the coast of Morocco. There, the ship would find the steady **trade winds**. Then it would ride the "trades," as sailors called them, across the ocean.

The second day out from England dawned with a ripple of wind. The executive officer, the ship's second in command, looked at the captain. At McGowan's nod, he picked up a megaphone and ordered the crew to set sail. "All hands!" he cried. "Lay aloft, lay out, and unfurl!"

The crew raced up the rigging and went into action. As soon as the sails were set, McGowan could see that there was a messy problem. The line that had been fitted in Bremerhaven was still new—stiff and full of kinks. In an instant, the *Eagle*'s new lines had knotted themselves into rats' nests.

McGowan quickly ordered the sailors to take down the new lines one by one. Kinks were shaken out and lines were straightened. Then, under sail at last, the *Eagle* moved forward under the power of the wind.

It was a sight to admire—and not just for the *Eagle*'s crew. Other ships coming within sight of the square-rigger changed course and rushed closer for a better view of the majestic vessel.

The *Eagle* arrived at Madeira carrying full sail. As it neared its anchorage, the command was passed: "Lay aloft...lay out...and furl!"

In minutes, the job was done perfectly—even in the dark. The *Eagle* had completed its first ocean passage. The inexperienced crew had become sailors—and so far the voyage had been smooth.

After two days, the *Eagle*'s crew was rested and the ship's hold was full of food, fuel, and other supplies. Then the *Eagle* was off again. This time, it was bound for the island of Bermuda.

A half day out of Madeira, the *Eagle* picked up the trade winds. Carrying full sail day and night, the ship swept through the tropical sea. Its masts stretched skyward and its sails stood out white against the blue-green sky.

With the trade winds blowing steadily from the east day after day, the crew hardly needed to touch the sails. As square-rig sailors had done for hundreds of years,

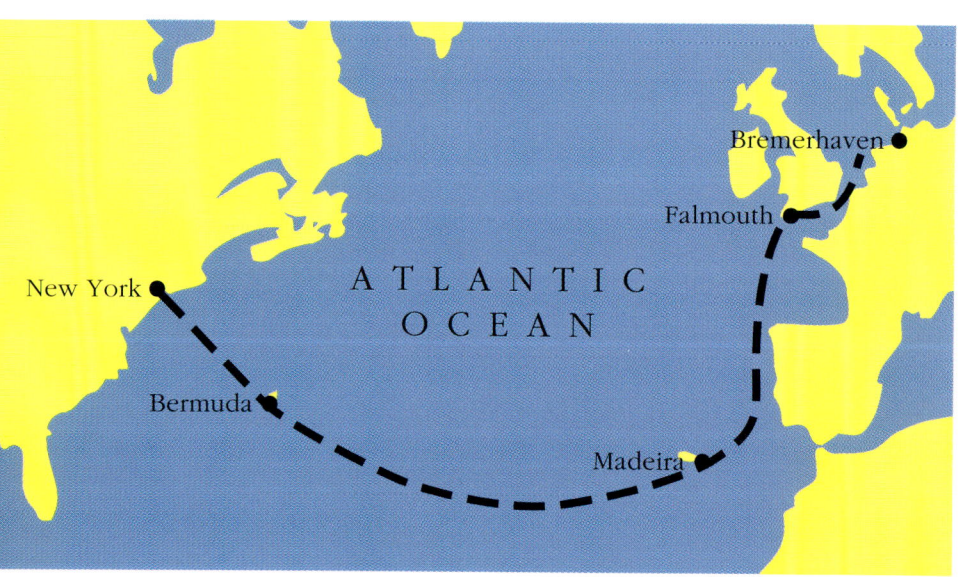

The *Eagle* rode the trade winds across the Atlantic.

the *Eagle*'s crew let the trade winds carry them across the Atlantic.

With time free to explore the *Eagle*, the crew discovered the brass and the teak wood that had been painted over during the war. Little by little they stripped off the paint, carefully polishing the brass and varnishing the wood.

As the days passed, the *Eagle* began to gleam in the sunlight. Even the sails began to flash whiter as they became bleached by the tropical sun. By day, crew members worked or sprawled in the sun. By night, songs — in English and German — drifted up from the crew's quarters.

Except for a spell of calm weather, when the *Eagle*'s engine carried it along, the trip to Bermuda was a perfect voyage. Then, after a few days of celebrations and parties on that island, the *Eagle* was back at sea, bound for New York.

From the start, though, McGowan was uneasy about this final leg of the journey. He could not put his finger on it... but something seemed wrong. Pacing the deck, he nervously scanned the sky and the sea as captains had done for hundreds of years.

Feeling tense, he went to his cabin around midnight — only to be roughly awakened a few hours later. The *Eagle* was lurching through the dark sea, and the crew was rushing about, working feverishly to get the ship

Eagle sailors have worked and stood watch through many storms.

under control. Racing to the deck, McGowan looked around and realized what was happening. A hurricane was on the way.

All morning the crew raced against time to prepare the ship for the approaching storm. The sailors put extra lashings on the small boats and other loose gear. They rigged extra lifelines and fastened down all hatches and doors. Meanwhile, the *Eagle* raced on, sails on the foremast and mainmast, trying to run ahead of the storm.

As the hours passed, the weather—and the sea—grew rougher. Normally, two sailors worked the ship's huge wheel. Now, though, the sailors were struggling just to hold on to the wheel. Huge swells of water were coming up from behind. They smacked the ship's rudder with such force that it nearly swept the helmsmen—the sailors working the wheel—off their feet. McGowan put two more sailors on the wheel and hoped that would be enough.

As the storm increased in fury, the waves became ever larger. In a short time, eight sailors were working at the wheel. All day, the captain stayed on deck. Watching the seas and steering the ship this way and that, McGowan kept the square-rigger running away from the storm.

The worst, however, was still to come—as McGowan well knew. Fierce blasts of wind started to turn the waves into explosions of spray that hurled through the air with violent force. The wind bellowed and shrieked at speeds of more than 60 knots. The ship began to plunge and wallow in the furious sea.

Then, suddenly, all eyes turned aloft as a sharp tearing sound—the ripping of fabric—momentarily drowned out the howl of the wind. The upper and lower topsails on the foremast were the first to go. One moment they were straining in the wind. In the next instant, they had vanished. In their place were only ragged ribbons of cloth, whipping furiously in the wind.

As the ship tore through the water, the force of the wind shredded more sails. Soon, only two were left.

McGowan knew there was only one thing to do. The ship would have to heave to—to turn so that it would go with the wind of the storm. Turning the ship like this would be safer for the vessel. But it would mean that the *Eagle* had to go wherever the wind drove it—for as long as the storm lasted. And making the turn was dangerous in itself. There was a good chance that the *Eagle* would be swamped by an oncoming wave.

Issuing his commands, McGowan readied the crew for the maneuver. Then, seeing a gap between giant waves, he ordered the sailors at the wheel to turn as fast as they could. Using all their strength, they forced the wheel—and the mighty ship—around to its new course.

In an instant, a wave bore down on the ship, bringing a towering cliff of water

On the *Eagle,* sailors have always gone aloft, even in the worst weather.

smashing down on the deck. Instead of bucking and plunging, though, the ship—all 295 feet of it—bobbed up and over the crest of the giant wave. The *Eagle* was safe—for the time being.

With the ship hove to, the crew didn't even try to steer. They simply lashed the wheel in position and left it alone.Hour after hour, the ship moved on. The storm moved, too—but faster. By sunset, the storm had passed. The crew could relax. The *Eagle*—battered and torn, but still afloat—would be in New York the next day.

As the ship entered New York Harbor, its new sails were in shreds. And it was powered by its engine, not by wind and sails. But the *Eagle* carried its wounds proudly. Tested by the worst the sea could offer, the *Eagle* had proved itself and its crew. Both the captain and the crew knew that the *Eagle* was ready to take its place in the long tradition of the sea.

CHAPTER 6

AT SEA WITH THE *EAGLE*
NEW YORK
1994

In the years since that voyage across the Atlantic, the *Eagle* has made dozens and dozens of journeys. It has visited cities from Boston, Massachusetts, to Sydney, Australia. It has appeared in spectacular festivals with other tall ships. And it has even made a year-long, around-the-world voyage that took it to places it had never been before.

Wherever it has gone, the *Eagle* has drawn crowds of admirers. Some are sailors themselves, eager to see the ultimate in traditional sailing ships. Others are history buffs, people who love the objects and the ways of the past. Most visitors, however, come out of curiosity, just to see firsthand an old-fashioned square-rigger like the ones they have read about in history books and storybooks.

No matter why they come, though, visitors are always amazed at the sight of the gleaming white ship. And they

The *Eagle* has made many dramatic entrances into New York Harbor.

The *Eagle* has raised its sails near the coast of England, too.

almost always feel something of the spirit that keeps the *Eagle* alive.

Over the years, the *Eagle* has been modernized in important ways that make it safer and easier to sail. State-of-the-art computer systems now help the crew's

President John F. Kennedy was one of many distinguished visitors to the *Eagle*.

navigators. Power-driven winches can be used to raise and lower sails in emergencies or when the crew is shorthanded. Beds have replaced the hammocks that once were the sleeping places of the crew and cadets. Even television sets have been added, to the delight of the *Eagle*'s crew.

Beneath it all, however, the *Eagle* remains much as it was, a sailing ship powered by the wind and by the hands and hearts of its crew.

And this makes the *Eagle* the special ship that it is.

Over the years, the square-rigger has been a school for thousands of Coast Guard cadets. It has also been a workplace for the permanent crew that serves on the ship full time.

For these men and women, the *Eagle* has been more than just a temporary home at sea. It has been a place for them to learn the ways of the sea. It has also been a place to test themselves against the elements that can make the sea one of the most dangerous places on earth.

Most of all, though, the *Eagle* has been a place where people share a way of life that goes back hundreds, even thousands, of years. Hauling the lines, working aloft in the rigging, navigating by the sun and stars are all part of the experience. But so is the way in which the *Eagle* connects people to the past, helping the men and women of the

Few visitors have ever forgotten the sight of a square-rigger under sail.

The *Eagle* has carried on a sailing tradition that goes back hundreds of years.

Coast Guard carry on age-old traditions of the sea. The *Eagle* is a ship that brings people together—as shipmates in the struggle to survive the many joys and dangers of the open sea.

GLOSSARY

aloft ♣ Up in the rigging of a sailing ship.
barnacle ♣ A small, shelled saltwater creature that attaches itself to rocks, ship bottoms, and docks.
barque ♣ A three-masted sailing ship; short for barquentine or barkentine.
bow ♣ The front of a ship.
bridge ♣ The raised area of a ship from which the captain commands.
cadet ♣ A young man or woman in training for one of the armed services.
cleat ♣ A small wooden or metal block for fastening lines on a ship.
fore t'gallant ♣ On a square-rigged sailing ship, a sail located on the fore, or front-most, mast. (See diagram on page 10.)
hands ♣ The sailors, or crew, of a ship.
hull ♣ The body of a ship.
knot ♣ A unit of speed used for ships equal to 1 nautical mile (6,076 feet) per hour.
mess ♣ A group of people who regularly share meals, usually in the armed forces; also the place where meals are eaten.

mine ⚓ A floating object loaded with explosives; in warfare, mines are used to block and destroy enemy ships.

old salts ⚓ Experienced, old-time sailors.

plot ⚓ To figure out a ship's current position or the way to get to another place.

spoils of war ⚓ Treasures and materials that a defeated country must give over to its conqueror.

stern ⚓ The back of a boat.

trade wind ⚓ A steady wind blowing toward the equator; found from about 30° north of the equator to 30° south of the equator.

wallow ⚓ To roll about.

ward room ⚓ On shipboard, the area in which officer's eat and/or relax.

watches ⚓ On ships, the period of time during which people work at a particular task. Traditionally, sailors stand, or have, 4-hour watches.

wear ship ⚓ To move the yards and change the angle of the sails on a ship; usually done to keep the wind in the sails when the wind changes or when the ship needs to change direction.

wheel and deal ⚓ To trade and operate sharply and cleverly.

FURTHER READING

Aust, Sigfried. *Ships! Come Aboard*. Minneapolis, Minnesota: Lerner Publications, 1992.

Chapelle, Howard I. *The Baltimore Clipper: Its Origin and Development*. Mineola, New York: Dover, 1988.

Chapelle, Howard I. *History of American Sailing Ships*. Avenel, New Jersey: Outlet Book Company, 1988.

Durant, John and Alice. *Pictorial History of American Ships on the High Seas and Inland Waters*. New York: A.S. Barnes, 1953.

Ward, Ralph T. *Ships Through History*. Indianapolis, Indiana: Bobbs-Merrill, 1973.

INDEX

Allies, 13, 23
Atlantic Ocean, 19, 26, 28, 32, 38
Bermuda, 31, 33
Boston, Massachusetts, 38
Bremerhaven, Germany, 15, 17, 19, 24, 27, 28, 31
Eagle, 5, 6, 7, 8, 9, 11, 12, 13, 24, 27, 28, 29, 30, 31, 32, 33, 35, 36, 37, 38, 40, 41, 43, 44
England, 13, 28, 30
Europe, 23
Falmouth, England, 28
France, 13, 23
Germany, 13, 15, 16, 20
Hitler, Adolf, 13, 15
Horst Wessel, 13, 15, 16, 17, 19, 20, 21, 22, 24, 25, 26, 27
Kennedy, John F., 41
Madeira, 30, 31
McGowan, Commander Gordan, 16, 17, 18, 19, 20, 21, 22, 23, 24, 25, 26, 30, 31, 33, 34, 35, 36, 37
Morocco, 30
Nazi Party, 15, 27
New London, Connecticut, 5
New York Harbor, 37
New York, New York, 28, 33, 37, 38
Normandy, France, 23
North Sea, 26
Soviet Union, 13
Sydney, Australia, 38
United States, 13
U.S. Coast Guard, 5, 13, 16, 23, 24, 25, 26, 27, 43, 44
U.S. Coast Guard Academy, 6,
Von, 22
World War II, 13